# Where The Light Enters

Holly Boyes

BookLeaf
Publishing

India | USA | UK

Presentation by *BookLeaf Publishing*

Web: www.bookleafpub.com

E-mail: info@bookleafpub.com

ISBN: 9789357444019

First edition 2022

# DEDICATION

"Not sure that I deserve all the Love that I receive, but I give it all to her"

-Billy Strings


Always for my sweet Abilene

# ACKNOWLEDGEMENT

Here's to the beginning of something to hold onto. Of all my wishes and dreams, mine is for ALL of humanity to catch a glimpse of their potential. Here's to many more!

Eternally grateful to my family for loving through the wind and rain.

Thank you CC MACK for everything you have taught me and continue to guide me through.

Thank you Jared for allowing me the space to grow and always showing me my reflection so that I may see the light.

# WORDS OF A FRIEND

Everything's going to get lighter,
even if it never gets better.

# NOW

Here is the beginning
Start now
Here is the beginning
Ask how
Here is the beginning
It's over now

# PONDER

Sometimes I wonder
what is holding me

What will hold you
if you can't be held

What will show you
if you have not seen

What will open you
Who will open me

# COSMIC

There is no vail
Nothing to hide behind
You're too bright anyway

Too bright to not be
Seen
Heard
Loved
Respected
Admired

You are
I am
Seen
Heard
Loved
Respected
Admired

Flow free from fear fast
Free free free at last

# BLAME



I don't blame you
Nor resent you
My brain isn't wired for that shit
I have been blessed with forgiveness

# NEW

Bring it back to ground level
Smash all the pieces
So many different ways of seeing
Infinite possibilities of feeling
How could it ever be the right one?
When did it start to matter?

What should I let go of?
Injustice and imbalance

# DONT EVER STOP

I honor my emotions
And my feelings are always valid

I am worthy of Love, Respect, and Happiness
I honor my well being

And in doing so for those around me
I will be in content as those gifts are returned to
me - not from them, but myself

# TOMORROW

Tomorrow will come
And a new day will appear
However it will still be today

Morning has come and gone
I no longer mourn the early hours
Nor do I wish the mourning well

THIS IS A RISE - NOTHING LESS

# TODAY

Today is where I draw the line
I have slept on this opportunity
A bed of layered of blood sweat and tear

No longer is this pain mine

# WHEN WILL WE

Stop to understand why
And then forget to ask

Live enough to Love
And then forget to hate

# EVERYTHING CHANGED

I'm moving on
You can't keep me here

I'm moving on
It will never be there

I'm moving on
The time has changed

I'm moving on
With only myself
To blame

# SETTELING DUST

At first it was a blinding sight
And then The Promise Land appeared
For so long I have waited to see
Waited to see what has always been there

# SUMMERTIME I

13

The heat pressing against your skin
Slowly then suddenly piercing your layers
Slightly pinkish tone appears from inside

Your excitement makes you feel like floating
Maybe you're a ballon
Swelling cheeks and cheesy grins
Now rosey all over

# SUMMERTIME II

14

Water and sunshine
Sun and sweat together
As Summers love sauce
Salty and vital

# CHOAS

Empty Absolute heartbreak.
Momentum unstoppable.
River rising, ships capsizing.

Drowning in rain of unspoken words-
umbrella unnecessary-
happiness contrary.

Speeding on resent
Light-years from content
Crying out loud
Stuck in this cloud
a sheet of regret
that adorns this body of defeat

Lift my eyes to meet the guise
of what is unreal
what's left
not to Feel


Lift my eyes- again
to meet the guise of what is Real-
Telling all of what's left to Heal

Look through the window of fate
Make yourself a mighty wide gate
Coming in like the red eye flight
Trailing then disapearing into the night

Feel Your Feelings

WORDS HAVE NO MEANING
FEELINGS HAVE NO FEELING

diving deep into fear and shame
all that's left in my name

dive deep into the pain
what's left the reign
dig it up- take the gain

the strength to be found
when only you are around

dive deep into the pain
give what's left the reign
dig it up & take the gain
after all is done
its Name

The strength to be found when only you are
around- prepare for leaps and bounds
You'll feel the sound.

The sound of breath singing the pitch of
untainted ease... be here now
Feel the REALEASE

When you're up and feeling high
don't forget to touch the sky
tomorrow's never promised
let all your fear be dismissed

who knows how many time
it will go before you allow it to flow-
Flow into your hearts center...
a heart as wide as the river
Flow into Gia widest river

Don't let go of ALL you No
for the NOing will find YES
One day it will no longer guess
Put it to the test
Disturb the unrest

Limited love lacking respect
will only bring limitless regret

# FLOWERS AND RAIN

My mind asleep in a quiet séance
As my body wakens
 for her sensual chaos
She is the essence of a powerful storm
Her kisses feel like rain on a heart scorched
Her eyes striking like flashes of lightning
As clouds of passion roll across to excite me
Our souls come together with such passionate
pressure
She drenches me with erotic pleasure
Raining down love all over my body
Tenderly caressing with a touch of naughty
With a love so strong reckless and relentless
She rages on like a violent tempest
A crack of thunder deep within my core
My body trembles through the downpour
Just like the storm I knew she'd blow away
But I will wait for her like the flowers do the
rain

# WITH OR WITHOUT

With or without her

Is she everything I've ever dreamed
Or is my mind playing tricks on me
Is she more than just a friend to me
Or is she a lifelong fantasy

Does my heart really want for her
Or is she my soul's dream from before
An imagining of my past I longed for
Or does she represent so much more

Are her feelings real or is she on the take
My heart cannot withstand another break
But For a love so unimaginable it makes me
ache
I guess it's a chance I've got to take

Life without her just isn't the same
But is she worth all the future pain
Years of tears falling like rain
With her or without her...I'll go insane

# PLAY ME

Profound sensation yet calming me tearfully
Like a work of art so beautiful so captivating
As if painted with angelic divinity
Drawing whispers of air till I'm no longer
breathing
Experiencing a level of impassioned sensuality
It's everything my soul always knew it would be
A sobering intoxication of supremacy
Like a musician tuning my body masterfully
Capturing my heart lyrically
Playing an overwhelming song of ecstasy
Orchestrating orgasmic crescendos so easily
She conducts my heart as she sings to me
I've never been moved so beautifully
Touched by grace so soulfully
Like the impact of a bomb dropped lovingly
Exploding shrapnel of pain from my body
Releasing from chains the song within me
Now together we'll sing in harmony
Until the tides no more are pulled by gravity
She'll dwell in my soul forever to be
My lasting love for eternity

All the years you so desperately ached
From all the ones that made you wait

All the fears you never hope to escape
From all the times your heart had to break
All the loneliness you feel when you wake
From all the ones you had to forsake
All the loyalty that you misplaced
From all the ones whose truths were fake
All the memories you never made
From all the love you didn't make
Can't even compare to the soul-wrenching pain
That in all the lost chances and all the mistakes
I'm not one you're willing to take
-CC MACK

# ALL IT TAKES

All the years you so desperately ached
From all the ones that made you wait
All the fears you never hope to escape
From all the times your heart had to break
All the loneliness you feel when you wake
From all the ones you had to forsake
All the loyalty that you misplaced
From all the ones whose truths were fake
All the memories you never made
From all the love you didn't make
Can't even compare to the soul-wrenching pain
That in all the lost chances and all the mistakes
I'm not one you're willing to take

-CC MACK

# STOP

Stop and listen
Context does not matter
Attachment caused intention

You are the only one who can do this
No one else is going to know your
Attachments or Intentions

# MOTHER OCEAN

Mother Ocean i seek your solice.
I come to get my mind right.
To witness the sun bring me a new day.
To rest my weary soul upon your shore
To surrender to the  music of the waves that lull
me  into that part of myself I don't visit enough.
To let the breeze blow away all the cobwebs in
my head
To let the sand polish me back to my shining
self.
To watch the birds to remind me I can fly.
To learn to ebb and flow like the tides
To ponder the shapes in the clouds and the
stories that they tell
Yes Mother Ocean, I came to get my mind right.
You never let me down.


-Gemma/CC MACK